WALTZING WITH HORSES

Waltzing with Horses

Poems

FELICIA MITCHELL

Felicia Mitchell

Press 53
Winston-Salem

Press 53, LLC
PO Box 30314
Winston-Salem, NC 27130

First Edition

Cover design by Kevin Morgan Watson

Cover art, "Wild Horse Can't Drag Me Away," Copyright © 2013
by Igor Svibilsky, used by permission of the artist.

Author photo by Angelia Denise Stanley

Printed on acid-free paper
ISBN 978-1-941209-08-0

for Guy Benjamin Mitchell Love

Acknowledgments

Grateful acknowledgment is made to the editors of the following journals in which poems noted first appeared:

A! Magazine for the Arts, "In My Dreams," "Specimens"; *Antietem Review,* "Scuppernong Jelly"; *Arrowsmith,* "Let Me Draw You a Picture"; *Artemis. Artists and Writers of the Blue Ridge and Beyond,* "First Love," "Revelation at Philpott Lake"; *Blood Orange Review,* "Album"; *Blue Fifth Review,* "Eight Below"; *Blueline,* "More"; *Columbia: A Journal of Literature and Art,* "Venus of Meadowview"; *Coping with Cancer Magazine,* "Knitting in the Chemo Room"; *The Dead Mule School of Southern Literature,* "A Bird in the Hand," "At the S&S Cafeteria," "Ducks," "Fairy Stones," "I Remember Biscuits," "The Lost Language of Dragons," "Marvelous," "Poem with a Camel in It," "Sleeping with Apples," "Thanksgiving," "There Is No Map," "Waiting with Crows," "Wake Robin," "Wateree Swamp"; *Earth's Daughters,* "Out of the Picture"; *Elohi Gadugi,* "Bamboo Loops"; *Fire,* "The Angel of Death Disguised as a Park Bench"; *Fresh Ground: A Poetry Annual,* "Bone"; *the Kerf,* "Like Herding Chickens," "Waltzing with Horses"; *Kudzu Literary Magazine,* "Near Eve"; *Hospital Drive: A Journal of Word and Image,* "Paris"; *Manzanita: Literary Journal of the Mother Lode and Sierra,* "Genesis"; *The Medulla Review,* "Pangaea"; *Oregon East,* "After the Fall"; *Oyez Review,* "Iron Mountain Trail"; *Pinyon Poetry,* "Sunburst"; *PMS.PoemMemoirStory,* "Where Are My Daughters?"; *Potato Eyes,* "My Country Garden," "My Mind Has a Body of its Own," "When Wild Hart Cherries Are Too High To Pick"; *Potomac Review,* "Gone To Seed"; *Referential Magazine,* "My Turn Out of the Box"; *River Poets Journal,* "A Day without a Poem"; *R-KV-R-Y Quarterly Literary Journal,* "How To Walk Down a County Road"; *Southern Women's Review,* "The Other Night at Grace Healthcare & Rehabilitation"; *Sow's Ear Poetry Review,* "Borscht"; *Sugar Mule Literary Magazine,* "Bear Calls," "Rorschach Blot"; *Terrain: A Journal of the Built & Natural Environments,* "Bat Moral";

"Dirge"; and "Near Penland"; *Weber Journal*, "Bird in Flight"; *Wild Goose Poetry Review*, "A Certain Slant of Light"; *A Wise Woman's Garden*, "Diana"; and *Xanadu. The Long Island Poetry Collective*, "Dove at the Window."

Grateful acknowledgement is also made to the editors and publishers of these poems that have appeared previously in anthologies: *Back to Joy*, edited by June Cotner (Andrews McMeel Publishing, 2014), "More"; *Low Explosions. Writings on the Body*, edited by Casie Fedukovich with Steve Sparks (Knoxville Writers' Guild, 2006), "Missing"; *Rough Places Plain. Poems of the Mountains*, edited by Margot Wizansky (Salt Marsh Pottery Press, 2005),"When Wild Hart Cherries Are Too High To Pick"; *The South Atlantic Coast and Piedmont: A Literary Field Guide*, edited by Sara St. Antoine, Trudy H. Nicholson, Trudy Nicholson, and Paul Mirocha (Milkweed Editions, 2006), "My Country Garden; and *Sunrise from Blue Thunder*, edited by Ami Kaye (Pirene's Fountain, 2011), "One Green Heron at Dusk."

Some of the poems also appeared previously in chapbooks: *The Cleft of the Rock* (Finishing Line Press, 2009), *There Is No Map* (The Dead Mule School of Southern Literature Online Chapbook, 2008), and *Earthenware Fertility Figure* (Talent House, 1999, a winner of the 1999 Talent House Chapbook Competition). "Up from Tumbling Creek" won a 2011 Poetry Society of Virginia Public Metrorail Art Project Award. "In the Realm of Grass" was written for Bud Caywood's painting of the same name and featured in a show of his work entitled "Encaustic, Ekphrastic" (Hickory, NC, Bethlehem Branch Library, 2011). "The Angel of Death Disguised as a Park Bench" is based on a work of art by the same name crafted in steel and mahogany by Sylvie Rosenthal in memory of Albert Huffstickler (2002).

Waltzing with Horses

III

IV

V

A Day without a Poem

On a day without a poem,
there is no need for meter—
just the beat of a heart or two
for good measure.
And instead of rhyme,
one bird can call after another.
On a day without a poem,
there is no imagery.
The sky is blue.
The clouds are clouds.
On a day without a poem,
there is no journey motif,
only a journey up and over rocks
and through woods and meadows.
Climbing to the top of a mountain
is no different from climbing
to the top of a mountain,
nothing like climbing Mount Purgatory
to catch a glimpse of Paradiso.
You are not a poet.
The man you are with is not a poet.
You are just two people on a hike.
Hobblebush flowers on a mossy ground
on the top of the mountain
are white like white flowers,
the moss as mossy as moss.
There is no symbolism.
When it is time to turn around,
it is time to turn back and walk
until you pause to waltz with wild horses,
without music, without rhythm,
in a field of wildflowers.
Perhaps words needs stanzas
no more than horses need pens
or dancers need a dance floor.
On a day without a poem,

when there is a full moon waiting
at the end of the trail,
punctuation is superfluous.
This day does not need a title,
although it is as tempting to give it one
as it is to press a violet
or a whole mountain of a day
between the pages of a book.

I

Specimens

My son traces the bird claw,
his left hand holding the black marker
like a magic wand that will fuse life and death
right in front of my skeptical eyes.

Upstairs, on my desk, my father's poems wait,
as fragile as the butterfly wings
pinned to my son's bedroom wall.

Each night, I slip upstairs to these poems.
I type their words, my fingers tracing my father's,
rhymes about swamps, night skies, and lost love
flashing fast and black on my computer screen.

On his desk, my son keeps a cat skull
in a box that delivered a Mother's Day orchid.

Sometimes we take it out and marvel at it.
I remember my son pulling it from a pile of leaves,
his hands holding up this perfect specimen.
I remember my mother handing me my father's poems.

My Mind Has a Body of Its Own

My mind has a body of its own.
You can see it crouched in shadows
of memories or wishes, like a cat
hiding from another fiercer cat
or taking sanctuary in a house
instead of taking chances in the woods.
Like a cat, it sleeps most of the time,
dreaming, dreaming, waking to eat.

Sometimes it wakes when I'm awake,
and the sound of this body colliding
with the body that actually pays rent
is enough to bring out neighbors
with pots of water and angry shouts
to stop the cat fight on my back steps.
Sometimes it slips away and prowls.
When it returns I towel its fur and
stroke it till it falls asleep again.

And when I'm quiet, like a mouse,
like when I'm dusting furniture
or sitting with a cup of coffee,
free of desire, I can hear a purr,
and if anyone asks I say
it's just the washing machine
vibrating again in the basement.

Bird in Flight

There is a bird nest
where other women would keep porcelain,
crystal, Hummel figurines.
Next to a child's plaster of Paris mask.
Above an old wallet.
Some ghost bird has been flying
in one house, or another,
for almost fifty years.
My mother is never lonely.
When a cricket sings in her house,
I hear about it in a letter.
Every time I visit,
I leave with another treasure:
colonial silver, blown glass water pitchers,
my father's frayed nightcap.
A bag of tomatoes.
She does not want us to clean house.
By the time she dies,
there will be little left: a bird nest,
an old wallet, lipstick on the bathroom counter.
We will bury the nest with her.
Her bird will fly.

Sunburst

Potato wagon thunder rolls
through the gray clouds
into my yard where branches snap and fall
like green beans into a basket.
In no time, there's enough water in the barrel
to wash my hair a dozen times.

When the rain stops falling,
I scoop it up and drink it with my hands.
Now the yard is littered, but the garden stands.
I can hear tomatoes sighing with relief.
A fig tree is getting up off its knees.

First Love

I read in my father's book
how Sappho loved Atthis
when the great oleander bloomed,
and growing up on Harbor Island
I loved life with just as much passion
as anyone on any Greek isle.

Oleander lined the streets, too,
where I ran and skipped and played,
some voice in my head reminding,
"These bushes can kill."

The ocean was a great unknown,
only to be entered, by permission,
when my mother was around.
Even so, I skirted it,
danced on the edge,
squirmed over jellyfish
and stared at any man-of-war
that washed ashore.

Only the Black-eyed Susans
could woo me back to dryer land,
their colors worth the trip
through the sand spurs
that separated the beach
from the sidewalks,
where oleander bloomed
all the way home.

Thanksgiving

It was the year we ate turkey
and a pot of black-eyed peas
with the good silver
that I will never forget
because it was my mother's birthday
and she wanted to apologize
for everything, not just the food,
but all we would let her do,
all any of the four of us could do,
was count out our blessings
like 42 imaginary candles
on an imaginary birthday cake
because we loved turkey
and black-eyed peas
and our mother.

Gone to Seed

If you wait too long,
the cauliflower on the hill
will burst into bloom
like an impatient wildflower.
No longer edible,
and barely photogenic,
it could be plucked from the face of the earth
to make room for something more useful

like another squash plant
or a cucumber or a tomato or a sunflower

or a rude awakening.
Better to pluck a cauliflower small but ripe
to eat it for supper
than to expect a miracle to grow
in your backyard.
If you pray too long over a ditch,
the water will never turn into wine
but will evaporate and come back as rain.

Album

1

In the photograph I do not take,
my father's feeding tube
feeds itself on his body:
the body that he has willed to outlast
every possible medical intervention.
And though he is not underground,
or lying in a wooden coffin,
there are flowers around his remains:
the Judas branch I snapped out front,
the hotel's daffodils, azalea blooms
from my mother's garden.
All of these fit in a Styrofoam cup.
All of my father fits in one bed.

2

In the photograph I do not take,
my father is not smiling
but his hand is waving,
its bandages white like flags of surrender.
He is waving at his grandson
whose yo-yo is a pendulum,
whose eyes are very sad,
whose note to his grandpa
written so precisely in a schoolboy's hand
is answered with the truth
by a man who cannot hear himself speak it:
"Not so good, Guy, not so good."

3

In the photograph I do not take,
my mother is out of the picture.
As much as she has seen, she has never seen this.
She has never seen quite this.

4

In the photograph I do not take,
nobody can see my cousin Walter
seated at the foot of the bed.
My father's companion since his death,
Walter takes up so little room
not even the night nurse mentions him
to her supervisor, or turns him in to God
for being AWOL from the hereafter.
Walter the politician has no pull now,
but he lets my father in on little secrets
and pulls the blanket over his toes.

5

In the photograph I do not take,
all my father's children are standing by
at the same time in the same room.
The black hair John pulled from our father's head
to mantle his own bald head is long.
Of all of us, he knows the most.
He knows how veins burn out and needles hurt
and nights are long when your roommate sleeps.
He knows how handicapped the healthy are,
how hard it is for them to focus
when they pass through the door downstairs
to halls that smell of old urine.
Our father knows that John knows the most
and holds the hand whose last pulse he counted.
The rest of us fan out like angel wings
on either side, waiting for a sign.

6

In the photograph I do not take,
I am crying tears like baroque pearls
in different, scattered sizes,
and the miracle is that they fall
painlessly from my tear ducts.
The camera is not on a tripod.
My arm is long enough, my fingers deft.
I can capture myself in time.
Later, I will string the pearls with silk thread
that looks nothing like a feeding tube.
I will wear them to my father's grave.
Another daughter might bury them.
I will wear them to my father's funeral
every day I wear them
and I will wear them every day.

Wateree Swamp

I remember how we left Mama
on a bedspread at the edge of the swamp,
nine months pregnant, with fried chicken to eat
and a shotgun to protect her from bears,
Daddy said, "bears" meaning "danger."

And she would have shot the gun too,
at a bear or a man or a renegade duck,
at anything that threatened her
or the child swimming inside her
while the other children and her husband
navigated a boat around cypress stumps
and looked for reflections in the water.

I remember that afternoon as easily
as I remember all our stories
and hold them as close as that shotgun
Mama held, or us, ready to pull them out
when I need them to protect me
from the idea that one day, some day,
nobody will know we left Mama
on a bedspread at the edge of a swamp,
nine months pregnant, eating fried chicken,
while her family disappeared into black water.

In the Realm of Grass

I believe a leaf of grass is no less than the journeywork of the stars.
—Walt Whitman

The grass will grow, the less you mow,
its mystery as radiant as a ray of sun,
its orbit less a lesson in phototropism
than a proverb read on leaves of grass.
The grass will grow, the less you mow.
What happens then, in this realm of grass,
where sunlight makes all colors possible?
Somewhere, across a fence, a neighbor gossips.
Just down the road, the sound of a riding mower
becomes as nagging as a guilty conscience.
Forget all that, forsaking the tidy for loose ends.
Look closely at what happens at your feet
when you are busy manicuring nature.
The grass will grow, the less you mow.
It is possible to stand on your grassy ground.
It is possible to stand on your ground.
I know how to stand my ground,
how to lay down the lawnmower,
how to forget the scythe rusting in the shed,
how to let grass lead me to quail and mice
and violets that bloom between its margins
like so many stellar thoughts.

Pangaea

You can see us here, drifters,
three entire continents of emotions
under one single roof. More, if you count
relatives scattered here and there like islands:

one grandma who speaks a foreign language,
the language of the old,
and a grandpa worn soft by nine decades of erosion.

Our edges are not as smooth as theirs.
Sometimes I feel like the Rock of Gibraltar,
both tourist attraction and gate to the underworld.
My words are as sharp as rocks.

Across the room, my son is a Florida key,
separated from me by 300 million years
instead of forty. I want to hold him
until he forgets I am made of flesh and bone.

My husband is nothing if not Antarctica.
The other day, I looked into his eyes and saw ferns.
Fossilized, they spoke volumes,
the words coming out of his eyes
instead of a mouth that clammed shut
as he watched his wife and son fight—
breaking plates as if they were just china.

There was a time when we were a supercontinent.
There was a time when I let the water crash at my feet,
inviting father and son to splash in it.

Look at us now, just spilling off the map.

I Remember Biscuits

This is how it begins,
the long decline to a time
when a sweet potato becomes a novelty
and bread crusts make a woman marvel
at the cleverness of bread.

Before milk turns to water,
or Brussels sprout to something inedible,
biscuits can make as much sense as newsprint.
Cooking up a pan is like opening your eyes
or shutting the kitchen door at night
and locking it before bed
and going to sleep in an old cotton gown.

There are some things a person can do
with her eyes closed, like pray or measure flour
or wait twelve minutes for biscuits to rise
in a hot oven.

And then she can't.
She just can't remember some things,
not where to write a row of numbers
or what to wear to bed
or how to put together four—no, five—basic things:
flour, salt, baking powder, shortening.
and milk.

It goes from there, it goes.

A person can live without biscuits.
Years can pass without numbers that figure
or sweet potato soufflé.
But I wish I could go back in time
to a day my mother remembered biscuits
and write everything down.

Bone

It could well be a mastodon bone
neglected all these years by hikers
climbing, but it's not, it's just
a hambone—neat and round—picked clean
more likely by dog than Neanderthal
though the cave that guards it
is dark and deep enough for secrets
and there's no telling just who ate
the ham and why and if it was seasoned
with honey or pepper and cooked
before the hiker bought it or grilled
on an open fire under a full moon while
I slept in a bed inside a frame house
and dreamed of sleeping in a cave
and eating meat cooked by a man
with hands large enough to wield a club
or to crush my skull like a nut.
If I step a little farther in, the cave
will make me stoop and I will hang
my arms and swing my hair and wait.

Elegy for My Grandmother

All the way to the family reunion,
phlox from my mother's garden
fills the car with a pink scent
reminiscent of sun and bees
and the sweet, sweet pain
of memories adrift like pollen.
These are memories I will lay
on my grandmother's grave.

I never knew my grandmother
but have visited Sandy Level
more years than she lived.
I remember her for her daughter.
Who will, one day, remember me?

My mother no longer tends her garden.
Sometimes she picks at violets
growing on a windowsill
and sometimes she calls me Mother.

II

Waltzing with Horses

After you've climbed to the top of the world,
or at least to the top of Virginia,
the only place to go is down and down again—
even if it means climbing over the same rocks
and navigating the same trail backwards
while carrying a heart as heavy as your backpack
because the hike will end just like a day or a book.

But there is more than one way to write an ending.
In one, you're waltzing in a meadow,
wild horses watching you and your partner.
Night comes and goes, and comes and goes again,
moon waning, Devil's Paintbrush gone to seed.
The ending is that there is no ending, only the dance.

In another, there is a full moon, and you're in your car
heading north on the highway instead of south
while moonlight like hobblebush petals falls softly
on the side of the road, illuminating a familiar trail.

Either way, you realize, there is a reason to come down.

Revelation at Philpott Lake

For George Byrd

I don't think the soul leaves the body;
it has to be the other way around,
the way a berry leaves its bramble
or a bird leaves its nest.
It has to feel a little like I feel
after I swim and I leave the water,
my arms leaving a whole lake behind.
What if the body leaves the soul
to give the soul more room to wander?
What if the soul is thankful,
hovering, a dragonfly over water?

A Bird in the Hand

When the cat delivers a bird,
I become human again—
holding a tiny creature in my hand
where I feel its heartbeat
and remember how it is
to be held, too, by somebody
whose heart is as soothing
as a mother's has to be to a child
curled on her breast, half asleep,
marking time with each thump,
each systole and each diastole—
each rhythm reaching further back
to the mother who came before
the mother who came before.

The quickening pulse between us
as startling as blood in a bird's beak,
as startling as a human connection,
it is impossible to resent the cat
that has stolen a bird from the air
and delivered it to me on the ground
where I stand, my hand opening
as the bird's heart beats its last beat
and I remember what it means
to be so close to another body
that it is almost impossible to know
where another heart starts
and your own heart ends
until another heart stops.

A mother's love births all loves,
is what I want to believe,
even the love that dies in your hand.

Dirge

The cherry tree is gone,
its limbs hidden in the woods
so I won't see them and cry again
to save the blood-red fruit that I hold fast to each summer
like my own heart.

My heart is in my mouth now,
it wants to leap out and lie there writhing with me on the grass
next to the last of my cherries
until I am dirty and stained like a woman raped
like a forest.

How can a tree be too close to a house?
It's the house that should move.
Or the house could learn to coexist.
If cherries stain a roof,
or the limbs of a tree caress an attic,
that is no worse than murder.

Every summer, it's something:
the hacked wildflowers, the discarded tree,
the herbicide sprayed on the side of the woods.
I am not a practical wife.
I live like a wood sprite
while my husband civilizes everything else he can.

But phantom pain is real.
The tumor in my breast, the cherry tree in the backyard,
the tulip magnolia that would never bloom, the crabgrass,
the violets in the grass—I feel them all, all gone,
the impractical, the unnecessary, the excised.

One Green Heron at Dusk

That green heron needs a telephone pole
as much as I need a camera in my hand
but there it is—making do without a tree
or without fish that used to be in this creek.
Tomorrow it will fly somewhere else.
This evening, nothing is the matter.
Dragonflies fly, the green heron eats.

Straining my neck as it shifts its neck,
I am seeking the perfect image of this heron.
That is the one I will leave by the creek,
the pictures in my camera just shadows
of a time that has come and gone
like the fish that used to swim here.

Later, if I close my eyes and clear my mind,
I will see a green heron as patient as a green heron
without a camera lens between us.

Paris

Sometimes I don't want to go see my mother.
I want to stay home and mop floors,
clean out cabinets, and wear a facial masque.
I want to organize the refrigerator:
bird suet in one corner, cheese in another.

Once, rustling through the vegetable bin,
I found perfume in a zippered pink heart,
a vial of my mother's favorite, her very best,
something she gave me when she cleaned house
for once and for all, shedding herself of her past.

I'd forgotten about Paris, a perfect perfume,
the odor of roses and sandalwood kissing oranges
with undertones of moss and amber and laughter.
This was my mother's scent, the scent of a woman
who was not incontinent and who liked to dance.

It was the scent of evenings at the American Legion
with my father, when my parents could stand up.

I unzipped the bag and sprayed some on my wrist,
wearing perfume through the house as I pushed a broom
through a dust that accumulates when you're busy—
too busy to notice how tired you are of feeling sad.

Tracks

There are all kinds,
and all kinds of shapes,
and some lead to lairs
or beaver dams
and some lead to roads
that wind through
the mountains like veins.
Other take you into fields
past jimson weed
and last season's corn
where raccoons forage
for grains as yellow as sun.

Somewhere in the woods
beside the field,
beside the corn field
gone to weeds—
a brittle field,
with patches of color—
a deer that left its tracks
hides from hunters,
its tracks sunk with fear.
Somewhere else,
where nobody can see its tracks.
a heron flies out from a creek
into the air.

And we keep walking,
looking up and looking down,
watching the heron fly away
and watching how a fox
could be here and gone
before our feet kicked the dirt
from the parking lot down the hill
past the white blaze up it
to the red blazed trail
where somebody tied
a pink ribbon to a tree.

Genesis

When the lizard is dead in your son's hands,
and he does not believe in letting go, he can either
stand at the altar of his backyard tree fort
and offer it up to a god he isn't acquainted with
yet or decide to take matters into his own hands
and operate. "It was a girl," he will tell you later,
"so I gutted it and took out the eggs and buried them."
Lizard innards like turtle eggs in rich compost could
generate or mutate in his imagination, or yours.
It's entirely possible that whatever your son planted
will grow into something he has seen in the movies.
It's entirely possible that one morning you two will
open up the back door and look out at the
hundreds of baby lizards he has been waiting for,
expectantly, like a child who does not know
the facts of life or death but believes—beyond a shadow
of a doubt—that his skills are remarkable.

Dove at the Window

A sweet potato sprouted
in my mother's kitchen.
Its leaves were the lace
that did not hang at her window,
its purple tint the paint
she did not apply to walls.

There was often a dove
at the window that framed
every picture that ever hung
above her kitchen table,
where yesterday's paper
was a tablecloth.

There was a radio that didn't work.
My mother listened intently
to crickets living in the house
and to the music of her bones.

Poem with a Camel in It

The smallest is the size of a rabbit,
its fossils as fragile as an old woman with osteoporosis.
The largest, 15 feet, is too big for the old woman's room
even if it were not a fossil but a plush toy.
Plush toys are never all that skeletal.
They are the opposite of skeletal,
with padding and fur and comic-strip features
on the most realistic specimens.
A 15-foot camel, either plush or plastic, is not an option
for a small, shared room in a large, shared nursing home.
Bones from a museum case would fit better,
under the bed or in the closet or separated into piles
for each of the old woman's four drawers.
But that is no sort of camel for this old woman.
She can show you exactly what a camel should be.
If you mention archaeology or Egypt, forget it.
If you mention the desert, she will turn her head.
Ask her what a hump is, and she'll laugh.
Just show her the little yellow plastic camel
that lives in Noah's Ark and she will grab it
and make it dance and soar across the windowsill,
a camel with wings on its feet
flying over the heads of all the other toys.

Venus of Meadowview

My body was round once,
my stomach an inner tube
in the sea of my pregnancy.
Even my legs inflated
to keep me afloat with child
as I looked down and watched
my breasts drifting from
my center of gravity to my son's.
Now there is nothing left,
save a few ripples of flesh
and some silver streaks
that emerge when I bathe.
But I remember my belly floating.
I remember holding onto it for life.

Almost Easter

Shaking bone meal
from my bare hands
into the rose bed
where only one bush grows,
I feel as if I'm scattering
my father's ashes
all over again.

This month marks
the seventh year
my father has lain
in my garden,
his ashes in my hands
still as palpable
as bone meal or thorns.

Easter Sunday,
I will hide an egg
behind his ear.
Jesus will call down to him
to get up and play.
He won't.
But the rose bush
that is turning green,
this rose will sink its roots
a little deeper in the earth
and in a few months
drop its petals
like so many red tears.

After the Fall

The next time, the earth won't move.
God won't ask for hostages,
brothers won't have to spill blood or die.
No falling star will wait for a wish
as you stand staring at the evening sky.
The fish won't jump, the cows will come home,
and rain will fall again in Eden for you,
the first man anyone loved and left.
When everything is said and done, too,
you'll count yourself blessed among men.
You can be sure as snakes stopped hissing, though,
the first day won't be as easy as the next.
You'll stand surprised where I abandoned you,
amused and hurt to be given back your innocence
as if it were money you lent me to buy food.
You'll try to yell, you'll pay the piper.
You'd settle for hell, just to hold me longer.
But when you reach out with the same hand
that held the apple and rocked the cradle
and touched me in the small of my back,
I'll be too far away to listen to reason.
I'll be too far gone to reach in the hills.
It's for you, I'll leave peace in the valley.

Lethe

I did not drink of the river Lethe,
but I dipped my paddle in and out of it
and let the water fall across my arms.

As a mother mourns a lost child,
rocking the phantom in her arms,
so too had I rocked my memories
until my arms ached and I had to paddle
seven miles upstream
just to shake them loose from my muscles.

It was either the exercise or the water
that made me wake up the next morning
feeling as if I had washed away some sin
I didn't have a name for anymore.
It was on the tip of my tongue,
but my tongue was inside my mouth;
and my mouth was closed.

III

Let Me Draw You a Picture

When I look at you, I turn greener than grass.
—Sappho

Let's call my lust a flame azalea,
planted in the shade, slow to branch out,
but its leaves as green as the front yard
right after a long summer rain.

Or let's call my lust a Chinese peony,
planted in full sun, and you're the ant
that eats the wax; only a robin eats you
before the petals loosen into bloom.

Or let's call my lust the forget-me-not
by the front steps, so small even I walk past it
most days and never stop to remark
how the blue is the blue of your eyes.

How to Walk Down a Country Road

One. You don't really need a guide to help
You find the way. Just follow all the doves
That gather on the wires until you see
No more. Then you will know you've gone so far
There are no wires or houses. Two. Avoid
Advice that says to face the traffic when
You're on a curve. Look at those doves. They know
The difference between life and death is not
As easy as all that. It takes some sense
To cross the road when cars are tumbling down
Like cold, white water with no place for you
To navigate. Three. Lose the road. You don't
Know country roads until you've stepped aside
Into somebody's pasture or a stream
With rocks as smooth as wings on doves—or stopped
Beneath an apple tree and eaten one
To prove you could survive in nature if
You really had to. Four. Turn back before
Your time runs out. Five. The doves may look
As if they're watching over you. They're not.
The crows aren't either. Not the cows, the leaves,
The lines on asphalt separating gray
From gray. You're on your own. Find your way home
Alone and then you'll know exactly what
It's like to walk right down a country road.

Missing

My mother is missing a breast.
At Sunday dinner, no concentrated sugar allowed,
she pulls the fabric of her blouse and lets it fall
against her deflated chest.
                    And then she points to the other one,
the one not even I, her daughter, suckled,
the one poised there like a teardrop.
I tell her *they* had to cut it off, that missing breast,
and smile and point to her plate.
"Here," I say. "You'll want to eat your turkey."
But she won't eat this white meat
pulled clean from the bone, soft and tender,
only yellow pudding sweetened artificially
and one slice of a bright orange yam.

She wants to be like everybody else, my mother.
She wants it all: two breasts, a real dessert,
a daughter whose white hair does not surprise her.
She wants to find the words to tell me she wants it all.
She wants to know who *they* are.

In the top drawer of a dresser she does not use,
my mother's prosthesis has a life of its own.
Neither jellyfish nor boob nor recyclable,
it lies in wait.
                    One day, my mother will find her breast,
and she will want to play catch with it
or dress it up like a baby doll or eat it with a spoon.
"Here," I'll say. "You'll want to drink your milk."

Bear Calls

I hear them in the early spring,
bear calls up on the side of the ridge—
a sound reminiscent of robin
but as jagged as a tree stump
gnawed by beaver.
Just yesterday, I stopped in my tracks,
certain I was hearing a long-extinct bird,
or a very hoarse robin,
its call as large as a dinosaur's,
until I realized it was just another bear.
It saw me before I saw it.
This is what always happens.
Before I realize I am being blessed,
the bear turns towards its sanctuary
leaving me alone in the woods
looking up.

When Wild Hart Cherries Are Too High to Pick

When the tree goes wild
and shoots higher
than your house,
let the wind
shake the cherries
into the palms of your hands
as you face the woods
on the lookout for deer.

Tell your child
to pick up the good ones
strewn on the grass
while you wait for more
to drop from the sky.

If you plant the pits
he spits from his mouth,
you can start a new grove.
At night, instead of counting stars,
you can count seedlings
by the light of the moon
and sing out your blessings.

Sing loud, like a wood thrush,
get it out of your system.
He will outgrow your arms
as fast as the crow flies,
long before he learns
which path to follow
down the mountain and why
you loved him the most
with his mouth full of cherries.

Ducks

Now that we have driven
all the way here, from one end of town
to the very end of the other—
past an airport with small planes
and a restaurant with a giant chicken,
through traffic thick with cars
and one school bus stopping every mile—
she does not want to see the ducks,
the ducks that are just over the hill
in the creek by the trees near a sidewalk
that is so paved and so accessible that
I thought this trip would be a good idea.
And I want to see the ducks.

"Let's go see the ducks!" I say,
but she stares at the big green field
lying there like a vast wilderness
past a snake of a sidewalk.
She does not want to go see the ducks.

It's not enough that I want to see them,
or to stretch my legs while I push her wheelchair
and flex my arm muscles and soak in sun.
She needs to want to see them too.
And so we pause at the playground
where a girl is pulling a baby up the slide.
Both are laughing hard.

"Look at that!" my mother laughs.
And we watch these two children,
and they play on the slide, up and down,
and the sun starts setting over the ducks,
and the traffic on the road calms down
enough for us to get back in the car
to drive back up the road towards home.

A Certain Slant of Light

There is a certain slant of light
some winter afternoons
that oppresses
and there is another that delights,
like a pileated woodpecker
on the side of a tree
or chocolate-covered cherries
pulled out of a backpack
and handed out one by one.

More

I'm not sure how much more there is
than the promise of five small eggs
laid by a phoebe inside a carport.
One day, some of them will hatch
or none of them or maybe two or three,
and perhaps I will be there to see them
fly into the meadow beyond the yard,
or maybe they will strike out alone,
when nobody is looking, not me, not you,
and life will go on, no more sacred,
no less tragic, simply what it is right now:
a nest of phoebes with five small eggs
as fragile as any hope I can ever have
and as open to the possibility of flight
as little birds about to hatch.

When Asked to Describe My Chemo Rash I Say

My rash is not
the color of rhododendrons
blooming along the banks
of a creek in summer,
in memory, in time.
It is not the color
of that sunset bleeding
through pines right now.
It is more the pink
of a mushroom, I think,
pale, tinged with yellow,
and tiny pustules of white—
and also the color of a flower
that has not yet evolved
but is struggling
with its genes, unseen,
caught up in dead leaves
and damp soil
as it weighs the options
of being as pretty as an orchid
or blending into
the forest floor.

Fairy Stones

1

Lopsided wings,
an angel shrugging.

2

Chip on a shoulder
as big as a heart.

3

A cross to bear.

4

Study for a torso
to be cast in bronze.

5

Words in a matrix
as if in a maze.

6

Worry stone
with wings.

7

Stone tears.

Out of the Picture

In the museum she has made of her living room,
photographs of my mother's life are stacked and pinned
as if looking at them will take the place of memory.
Each time I enter the door, she points to another one
or the same one I saw the time before, or before that.

This is my father, here, before he got fat.
He's standing on a pier with a fishing pole in his hand.
He had the most beautiful eyes my mother ever saw.

She keeps her old boyfriends in a baggy on the bookshelf.

This is my mother in a bathing suit next to a man from Turkey.
They are lying on the sand and smiling at the waves
that have been lapping at their feet like time.

There are so many children and cats and dogs and children
and my little dog she never saw until she got a photo
I mailed to her a year after I sent it the first time to show her
Spot posed all black and white in some white, white snow.

This is Kitty-Boo in my mother's two-year-old arms.
The sepia tint of the calico cat in the arms of a tow-haired girl
doesn't look any older than the tear on the top corner .
See my bare-foot girl-mother in the dirt with her cat?

I have my own copy of a photo of the two of us at a café
we went to just last month, where a woman near us
took my camera and took a picture that made me realize
for the first time in fifty years that I do look like my mother.
Side by side, we share tentative smiles and furrowed brows.
In my mother's copy, she has cut herself out of the picture.

Who is that old woman with white hair and a tentative smile,
blue eyes gleaming, a night-light in her dark night,
and why is she as invisible as a vampire in a mirror?

Once, my mother asked me if I remembered my brother,
a bright-eyed boy in a striped shirt buttoned all the way up.
She remembers him, and she remembers that he died,
but she doesn't remember a day of the year he was sick.

Bat Moral

Sometimes a bat is just a bat.
It's not an omen, or a vampire,
or a rabid threat to your good health.
It's just brown, and lonely,
as confused as you are sometimes
when you turn to find someone
and he has turned another corner.
A bat can be as warm and fuzzy
as you want it to be, or cuter,
but it's still not a good idea to touch it
even when it ends up in the grass
wrestling your dog at four in the afternoon
when it should be hanging upside down
like a good bat in the rafters
or turning some corner to find the woods.
Bad dog, bad bat, I'm okay, you're okay,
but it's still not so good to fight,
not mammal to mammal,
not at four in the afternoon
over who or what belongs in the yard
or who or what should go which way
when there are so many paths to choose from.

Up from Tumbling Creek

Rhododendron roots laddered
up from Tumbling Creek,
so I grabbed one and then another
to climb back to the road
while my son shook his hands free,
bare feet skipping rock to rock.

Bamboo Loops

If a woman dances alone to the sound of bamboo, and there is
nobody there to see her, is she there—or is it just the dance?

First, the high note, a chickadee
on a thin green branch.
                       Which simply proves
that wherever you go, there you are. Like a woman
in a bamboo forest in the middle of an oak grove
                               In Virginia.
Then a little rhythm from the wind.
Enough to make you hear wind chimes
and flutes and rain and mockingbirds.
                       The sound of music,
a rustling leaf sound, a light percussion.
Echoes of hollow wood hitting hollow wood,
but looped- and layered.
                    Each melody independent.
Not one tree falling but many trees leaning over,
this way and that, as lithe as guitar strings.
Or a woman who becomes her dance.
                        A bird, its song.
Of this earth and not of this earth.
Crow cawing on measures ruled by bamboo lines.
                          And a beat
that originates inside bamboo and embraces oak.
The sound of soft blood rushing through a body.
A loud afterthought or hands clapping thunder.
                  Wind in front of wind.
Across and up high, a woodpecker working wood.
Not last, not least, the dancer bowing out of bamboo.
                     Soft steps in mud
imprinting more memories over the memory of rain.
One foot in front of the other, on the way out.
Finale, finally, then another call and response.
                  The woman still there.
But gone.

IV

At the S&S Cafeteria

The woman at the next table
wants her mother to use her right hand.
"Use your right hand, Mother," she instructs,
shifting the fork from one side to the other
while green peas spill into rice like punctuation marks.
Mother, seated in a wheelchair, does as she is told,
moving food to mouth without uttering a word.

The woman at my table, my mother, eats her turnip greens
and comments on the macaroni and cheese.
She says the same thing about her food each time.
Soon she will ask for a bag for her pecan pie
so she can take it out and eat it later.

What I do at times like these is eat my slice of sweet potato pie.
It is sweet as memories spilling from Mama's mouth,
stories that get mixed up between bites of greens
and cheese that could be cooked a little longer.
I listen to every word my mother says
and watch her watch the woman spilling peas.

Rorschach Blot

In the dream I paused,
touched my son on his arm,
and pointed to the sky.

Look there, I did not say,
silence our only chance
at communication.

We were on a path
in a wilderness area
where I had walked before
with my lover,
who was not his father,
when I saw a hawk lift a bird
from its flight.

The red-shouldered hawk is broad,
as swift as death.

The sky was blue
in the dream as in life,
the hawk silhouetted with its prey,
feathers spilling ink on sky
like a Rorschach blot
that I studied from the ground,
feet planted next to my son's.
I am not sure he looked
for more than a second,
what was poetry to me
more of an assault to him.

How do you tell a child
that this is the way to die,
snatched in midflight?
How do you tell him
That his mother is going to live,
and love, even if cancer kills her?

A hawk, a junco in its talons,
is one way to begin.

Diana

After a sketch by Rembrandt van Rijn

When the sun sets on your day,
you shed your clothes
and we see you like you are,
like we are.

You are no ordinary idol.

Your stomach sags,
its folds like ripples in the spring
you soak your feet in after the hunt.

Your flesh puckers,
imitating craters
on the moon that guides you.

Your hands reveal their strength.

You are the queen of every woman
who inhabits a mortal body,
who rejects the ideal
to live with the realities
of the flesh.

We worship you in the woodlands
where nature, unlike art, will never lie.

Borscht

The third day, back on the burner,
it boils like blood in a witch's cauldron—
the roots picked, hidden in my bowels,
their minerals coursing in my closed veins.
There's no double, no toil, no trouble,
to let it steam and hiss but I want more,
more than this red bled from beets,
shaded by tomato, carrot, onion, and potato.
I want a last supper from it, a real meal
sparing me from the plain and simple fact:
This soup we made is almost gone.
Tomorrow, I'll have to start over,
pull out the chopping block, make decisions.
Part witch, more magician now,
I shake white barley into red,
watch it spread and grow, a rhododendron
swirling like magic from the wooden spoon.

The Other Night at Grace Healthcare & Rehabilitation

The other night,
I lay next to my mother
and let my hair fall against her face.

She giggled when it tickled her nose
and reached both hands out,
as if to hug me,
but she grabbed my hair instead—

gathering one pigtail in each fist—

and laughed some more,
as if she remembered exactly
what it means to mother.

Sleeping with Apples

I'm worried about the bag,
and if she'll wake up with it around her head—
red apples scattered across the white sheets
of her new bed in a new home with special locks,
as if apples are the only thing that might escape—
but no, if she hasn't killed herself yet,
she's not going to do it with a bag of apples
so I let her keep it there under the sheet
next to her purse and false teeth.

Queen Pu-Abi went to sleep with apples too,
something nobody will ever forget.
Her tomb filled with agate and gold,
her body wrapped in beads and cotton,
would she need apples when she awoke?
Her jewelry and all her cats?

My mother, who wants to keep the apples,
has given me her diamond ring,
which sparkles like a whole vault of treasure,
and her fifteen-year-old cat, which won't survive her.

No need to make more room in the tomb.
Everything Audrey needs is right beside her:
four apples she will never eat,
the teeth she glues in her mouth on good days, and
a glass that magnifies everything she doesn't understand.

Knitting in the Chemo Room

On my lap, purple yarn and plastic tubes:
a tangled web of medicine,
the cord for my headphones,
knitting as necessary as Herceptin,
Taxotere, Carboplatin, sodium chloride.

Inside my head, antique music boxes play,
their melodies innocent of the detritus of cancer.
I listen to every note, each time I sit,
imagine myself inside a box, this music box,
wheels turning steel into brainwaves
I call infusion too.

My hands are sometimes still,
my feet on the recliner moving with a beat.
Most times, I hold onto knitting needles
that are nothing like the small needles that stick me,
their filament growing in my hands
instead of in a network of veins.
Chemotherapy pushes in, wool pulls out,
and the dancing girl inside my head
keeps spinning to music composed by people
who died before I was born.

There Is No Map

First Sophie wants me to find her house,
and when we get there she tells me no,

she wants me to help her find her mother,
so we head back down the hall and look

until she tells me she needs to pee,
at which point we return to her room

where everything suddenly looks reasonable—
more like a place to lay your head for the night

than the home that Sophie will never find,
no matter how often or where we look.

But she's okay with it once she settles down
and I leave, wondering how I'll find her mother

in this tangled web of halls and rooms
where I never know which corner to turn to find

exactly what everybody needs me to find
(like dead mothers, cabins burnt to the ground)

or if I should just walk out the front door
and forget about helping anybody find anything

since I am just as lost myself, in my own way,
as lost as Sophie is, every night, come sundown.

My Country Garden

The dog fennel transplanted
from the fields of Toogoodoo
to our backyard in town
snapped in my fingers
like beans in my mother's
as I inhaled the odor
that made my brother sneeze.

And the rabbit tobacco
made it to harvest,
offering a more pungent taste
than the honeysuckle blossoms
we sucked from the fence
or the vinegar and honey
my mother mixed to ward off colds.

Only the sound of quail
was missing from my garden
tucked between an apple tree
and our neighbor's boxwoods.

I remember making bird calls, though,
and hammering a fence of wood scraps
to keep the lawn mower out.

Stone Mountain

I know my father could have told me
why sap rises and why it seeps out of trees,
sticky on my fingers when I touch them,
or why a gun shot across a valley
is always louder when you walk alone.

But he isn't here right now, and I am,
a creek's whispers all I have to go on,
and so I listen to what it has to say
about sap and beetles and solitude
and everything else I wonder about
as I wander along this trail, miles to go,
my father's walking stick firm in my hand.

Fever

Five thousand blackbirds
fell from the sky,
and my fever broke, brittle boned.

Gray snow clouds gathered,
ice on my brow.
I raised my head higher.

Between the trees
between the slats of my blinds,
a blue sky emerged
behind brown leaves.

I lay in my bed, hurting,
trapped between my cells
and four walls,
the only way out a window
to a world where blackbirds were falling,
my fever breaking with ice on my brow,
a blue sky and brown leaves,
brittle boned.

Where Are My Daughters?

Where are my daughters?
The crows know.
They kidnapped them,
stole their voices, and
hid their little bodies in the hills.
Now caws are children's cries
mocking me from tree tops.

Every morning, tracking them,
I follow a raccoon's trail
down a path that leads me past sorrow.
Every day I go a little farther.
I am still a mother.
My milk drops like breadcrumbs.
One day I will find my daughters,
or they will find me.

Some mornings I think I see
little girls like scarecrows
dancing in the cornfield behind the trees—
their faces streaked with mulberries,
their skirts wet from wading in the creek.
They do not know they are lost.
When I run to them, they disappear.
Some mornings I find myself
hiding behind a large bull,
eyeing a calf at a cow's teat.

My milk drops like breadcrumbs.
One day I will find my daughters,
or they will find me.

My Turn Out of the Box

Abandoned by angels
we wait our turn out of the box.
                    —Scott Owens

I

This morning,
I put my fingers to good use,
playing my piano
instead of striking the keys
of my laptop,
and the notes lifted me
off the bench
not quite to heaven
but a little farther than I had been
from hell.

II

The first thing I did
when I woke up to the sound of birds,
before I played the piano,
was write down some words.
This is not what I dreamed,
I wrote, but how I felt as I dreamed.
I felt redeemed by my dream.

III

I always thought she hated me,
but since the dream all memories
of everything my mother ever did wrong
are rising above me
like steam off a hot sidewalk
after a summer rain.

IV

Time passes, perspective ticks and tocks,
but sometimes a hand gets stuck
at a certain hour, on a certain page,
everything I write as confused as angels
hovering over my house,
their ears peeled to hear instructions written
in the notes of my piano
lost in a cacophony of birdsong.

V

The mother in my memory
is not the mother who smiles at me
and points to my picture when I visit her,
drawing a line from here to there,
as if to say I know who you are,
I know who you were and will be,
forever and ever, Amen.

VI

Sometimes I play the piano
at my mother's nursing home,
the shape notes in old hymnals
so hard to read that I make mistakes.
My mother still cringes
when I hit a false note.
She still smiles when I don't.

VII

Since the dream,
I want to revise everything.
What used to be a story about a piano
held together with rubber bands
is becoming a story about trust.
What used to be a story about a broken nose
is now a story about what it means to be kin.
What used to be a story about my father
is now the truth about
my father.

VIII

From a tune by Mendelssohn
to the sound of music made by birds,
the ghosts of the past
are competing with the ghosts of the present.

IX

When my memories shift perspective,
the mother who hurt me
becomes the mother who protected me.
Even so, abandoned one too many times by joy,
I wait my turn.

X

Although he looks straight at me
in my mind's eye,
I cannot see my father through my eye's eye.
I only see my mother.

XI

My mother, my muse:
loved or hated or hated and loved,
you always stood by me,
from piano practice to adultery.
I will give it all back to you
in turn.

XII

Abandoned by angels,
I cannot ask the angels how they fly.
I will ask my mother,
whose language is the language now
of birds.

XIII

Mothers are always right.
Life does not have to be a tragedy.
It can be one short paragraph in a diary
written before you turn the light on one morning,
your hand holding a pen
like a torch.

Iron Mountain Trail

Bear Activity is reported,
but I don't see shit—no scat.
Behind me, a bird rustles
in the rhododendron.
I think it is a bird.
If I turn my head,
it might turn out to be a bear
or the ghost of my lover
digging his own grave.

The Angel of Death Disguised as a Park Bench

For Sylvie Rosenthal

It's time to rest,
to stop shuffling your bird-boned feet
down sidewalks and across streets
and through alleys
where others who look just like you
nod their blessings.

There's a woman with a chisel in her hand.
She wants to reshape your brow.
All those furrows could be alabaster-smooth.
One touch, and she will remind you:
there is rest for the weary.
Listen to the advice the world gives you.

The sparrow on your shoulder could be a sign.
The crow cawing at the sun could be just as right
as the cashier at the last coffee house you sat at.
"Will that be all?" she asked.
"That will be all," you said.

All all all all —the crow caws.
The sparrow shudders
In front of you, the woman with the chisel
points to a park bench.
She wants you to sit down,
to rest your bird-boned feet,
so she can reshape your brow.
Next to her, the angel of death disguised as a park bench
beckons you like a mother.
Your mother, or god, your god-like mother.

There is rest for the weary.
Have a seat and let the sculptor heal you.
By the time you leave this earth,
there will no trace of it in your flesh,
just one more statue in the park
encircled with pigeons who will never go hungry,
and sparrows.

Eight Below

After a photograph by Jenny Baker

I am trying to decide, here, now,
if I am as cold as in a dream

in which I am the only person
reflected in a mirror of snow

frozen in time like a photograph
and white as a ghost of a snow angel

made by a child who does not ski
but falls down instead to play dead.

What I decide is that a dream
can be as warm as I want it to be,

even when it is eight below
according to the gauge inside the box

where my heart pumps blood
until the snow angel animates

and I rise up out of bed
to shake the ice off my gown.

A dream is just like a mirror
reflecting one thing or the other:

a ground covered in ice and snow
where cold captures the imagination

or a horizon where mountains rise
and clouds too, like mountains,

give us something more to imagine
until we end up standing tiptoe

on a drift of snow to get a better look
at what we thought we could not see.

In My Dreams

I never get to be the mermaid.
I'm always the woman with two feet
standing on solid ground and waving out to sea—
or maybe I'm not only waving but also not drowning,
realistic to a fault and as unimaginative as a pair of flip-flops.
No poet ever needs to save me from myself.
Still, even I have as much imagination as a fable.

If I took the flip-flops off my feet, for example,
and felt hot sand move like inspiration as I splayed my toes,
I might need to jump in the water and wash off.
I might learn what it feels like to let loose just once.

I could splash, turning or writhing, writhing or turning,
twisting my torso until nobody noticed my feet at all
but stared at the last person anybody would ever expect
letting her hair down for once and for all in salt water
until the fronds of her braid become anemones
and her nostrils gills.

I think I'd write my own poem after I recovered.
I'd hate for somebody to watch me from shore and blame alcohol
when all a woman needs, really, is a little hint of rapture
before she finds herself in way too deep and
it's time to climb back out of the ocean,
feet ready to slip-slop back into flip-flops
while all that hair, as tangled by now as seaweed,
gets ready to symbolize one thing or the other.

Wake Robin

After the door closes,
and my mother goes back in—
back to nursing home halls
that frame her days,
back to her Noah's Ark—
the earth turns on its axis
and I leave the way I came in.

Earlier, in the car, her eyes shut,
my mother clutched her seat
while I pointed out tulips
I thought she would want to see
after a winter inside.

It wasn't until we stopped for coffee
that she opened her eyes and smiled
at three flowering pears.

When wind blew white petals
into the open windows of the car,
we laughed and held them in our hands.

Now my mother is back inside,
where she wants to be,
and I am outside, seeing things
she will never see now.

Trillium grows by a river,
five deer graze in an open field,
and a mallard in a parking lot
looks for another duck.

Marvelous

You don't forget some things:
Not the taste of a fresh tomato

cut into small pieces on your plate
and fed to you bit by bit, on a fork,

until you open your mouth wider
and speak a word that makes sense.

"Marvelous," you say, smiling,
coy with the memory of tomatoes.

As much as you have forgotten,
you don't forget some things:

Not how to share a bite of your past
pulled from a fork and held out,

a crumb passing from bird to bird
or from one mother to her daughter.

Like Herding Chickens

Herding emotions is like herding chickens.
One goes one way, and one goes the other,
and one trips you up right where you stand.
Sometimes, if you lean down, one crouches,
ready for you to pick it up and carry it home.

Herding chickens is like chasing dreams,
but it never seems like an impossible chore.
It is as natural as collecting eggs or shelling peas
or letting your emotions out of their coop
so they can run free in a big, big yard.

Now and then, emotions come home to roost
without any invitation whatsoever, no herding,
no need to chase them through the cornfield
or grab them before they end up eaten by a hawk.
They rest side by side, safe from coyotes and rain,
as safe as chickens sleeping together after dark.

The Lost Language of Dragons

i

I thought she'd like the blue color
of the little winged dragon I found,
but she frowned, confused, unable
to speak the language of dragons.

ii

I thought she'd like to go for a ride,
but she forgot how to get in the car
and fell sideways, limp like her dragon
until I showed her how to sit up straight.

iii

I thought she'd like to wear dry clothes
as clean and soft as a dragon's wings,
but she was almost impossible to change.

iv

I thought her poinsettia was thriving,
but she watered it with coffee and it died,
shriveling up on her windowsill,
extinguished with the memory of dragons.

v

I thought she would always love blue,
anything blue, like her husband's eyes,
like her favorite color, like her shoes—
the shoes she takes off only to shower—
but I was wrong about the blue dragon
with softly glimmering gold wings
living in exile on the side of a hospital bed
where this woman likes to rest, clothed,
wet or dry, day or night or afternoon.

Near Eve

Sometimes I am higher than a hawk.
Sometimes the hawks are higher,
circling me while I eat an apple—
alone, on a rocky summit, near trees—
and beetles click and clack over my shoulders
like Adam would, if he were here, chiding:
"Don't throw that core off the cliff!"

What My Son Sees

Towards the end of a long run,
my son sees things, his journey his imagination.
One time, he says, he saw a parrot
somewhere near Bedford.
He has also seen dancing bears,
black bears dancing on the Appalachian Trail—
not echoes of Grateful Dead bears
tiptoeing through a forest
but real bears, albeit imaginary.
My son has seen real live bears
and wild orchids too.
He has seen the sun rise and the night fall
and a moon so big it was a boulder
he had to clamber over.
He has run so far and fast
his feet separated from his mind,
his mind watching his body
the way I used to watch him when he was small.
Last time he ran a hundred miles,
he said, he saw his father smoking a pipe.
His father was standing on the edge of Coosa Trail,
his arms crossed, looking the way
he always looks.
And then, as he kept running,
my son ran into the arms of a tree,
and the tree hugged him, not vice versa,
holding him with its arms.
Later, we said, both his father and I,
on separate occasions, not knowing what the other said,
"The tree *was* hugging you."
That's what he needs, our son,
deep in a forest, sleep deprived, running and running
until he thinks he can run no more:
parents who believe in him and a tree that cradles him
until all the wild horses gallop by, one by one,
their hooves a heart beating.

Scientific Method

We left the bloodroot by the side of the creek,
its rhizome red against brown mud.
Earlier, when I dug it up,
scratching through soil like a conjure woman, I fingered the roots
and pulled lightly,
thinking kind gestures make a difference
even to plants.
When I handed the flower to you,
you explained the scientific method.
Nodding, I stared at the red at the base of this small flower
and tried to believe it was not a corpse but a harbinger of spring.
I imagined the whole world upside down:
blood red roots grasping at the sun
while white petals found ground water.
By now more rain has fallen,
and I'm sure our plant is no longer by the creek.
It's in water rushing over rocks.
It's my belief in the scientific method, drowning.
It's Ophelia floating downstream.
It's your hands reaching into mine
and taking something almost whole
and breaking it in two
to teach me a lesson I will never forget—
that the scientific method can yield as much poetry
as results.

Waiting with Crows

"That's not my mother,"
I mutter to myself—
as audible as crows
cawing above my head,
above her head,
that small old woman
wearing scuffs for slippers,
not edema socks with dirty soles.

The ambulance driver hears me.
The small old woman hears me too.
Even the crows hear me,
our voices crossing like leaves
on a blustery day, this day.

My mother, still en route,
is the only one who doesn't hear me.
And so I wait, worrying:
worrying about my mother,
worrying about the small old woman
who has arrived at the ER alone,
worrying about words.

Nobody's last thought should be,
"No, I'm not her mother."

And so I wait some more.
Crows keep me company,
their caws more than caws.
I stretch my legs to draw closer.
Somebody could be calling,
"You who are weary, come home."

You who are weary, come home,
or come to this hospital, now, right now,
wearing slippers or socks,
softly and tenderly, in an ambulance,
come home, mother mother,
come home.

Near Penland

After the memorial service,
we buried a salamander instead,
Sylvie picking it up with a leaf
after I spotted it in the road
with its brains oozing out.

We didn't really bury it,
we tossed it into some Queen Ann's Lace
on the side of the winding road
on the side of the mountain.
Anything more would have been obvious.

It was a bright red, the red of valentines.
It was as plump as a pair of lips.
It was the red of Jesus's words in a Bible.
You get my drift.
It was so red it was almost still alive.

Farther down the road, we saw a snake
turning into asphalt, a gray snake
ghost of its former black snake self.
It was past saving.
I took a picture of this dead snake,
Sylvie took her jacket off in the rain.

Scuppernong Jelly

Picking the grapes
in the early morning sun,
wild poinsettias underfoot
and mockingbirds perched
on the rusting fence
while my mother's straw hat
bobbed alongside my hands
as they plucked the golden fruit,
wasn't enough for a memory.
Picturing the gnarled vines,
her gnarled hands,
the way the bag sagged with grapes
does not depict exactly how
I felt that morning.

On my kitchen shelf, above the stove,
one small jelly jar gathers dust.
Sometimes, when I open the door,
the light falls at just the right angle.
I'll never eat it.

Author Acknowledgments

In 2011, a sabbatical from Emory & Henry College allowed me to compile an early version of this collection. During this sabbatical, I found quiet time to be inspired in Washington County, Virginia, where I reside, and at the home of my friend George Byrd in Franklin County, Virginia, where some of these poems began. The sabbatical manuscript, which I reworked extensively in the summer of 2013, could not have evolved without the vision of Terri Kirby Erickson, mentor and friend. Terri's guidance helped me to create a more interesting manuscript, and Kevin Morgan Watson of Press 53 shared helpful edits and other invaluable support during the publication process. I am also grateful to the Virginia Center for the Creative Arts in Amherst, where a 2008 residency allowed me to focus on poems about my mother. Finally, no poem I have written appears without honoring my first mentors: my parents John A. Mitchell and Audrey McClary Mitchell, and my friend Albert Huffstickler.

FELICIA MITCHELL was born in Sumter, South Carolina, in 1956, and moved with her parents and three brothers to North Carolina, where she spent her early childhood in Wilmington and Wrightsville Beach. In 1966, she moved with her family to Columbia, South Carolina, where she attended the University of South Carolina (B.A., M.A.) after graduating from Booker T. Washington High School. She spent four years working in Athens, Georgia, before moving to Austin, Texas, to get a Ph.D. from The University of Texas at Austin. In Austin, she became active as a poet and taught her first poetry workshops through the Texas Union Informal Classes program. Since 1987, Mitchell has made her home in rural Washington County, Virginia. She teaches English at Emory & Henry College, where she received the William Carrington Finch Award for Faculty Excellence in 2011 and the James A. Davis Faculty Award in 2013. In addition to publishing poetry and nonfiction in journals, anthologies, and chapbooks, she has written articles for journals such as *College Composition and Communication*, *Mid-American Review*, and *Poets & Writers Magazine*. Scholarly work includes *Her Words: Diverse Voices in Contemporary Appalachian Women's Poetry*, which she compiled and edited for University of Tennessee Press (2002).

Cover artist IGOR SVIBILSKY was born in Ukraine. As a child, Igor was fascinated by the work of the famous Russian painters Ivan Aivazovsky, Ivan Shishkin, Isaac Levitan, and Valentin Serov. Their lyrical, sad, and poetic work played a significant role in the forming of Igor's vision of surrounding nature. His journey into the world of photography started when he got his first camera at age of seven. Igor experimented with watercolor painting, but photography became his primary media of expression. He is a self-taught photographer, but many classic and contemporary photographers have influenced him over the years, empowering him to create his own style.

Igor has exhibited extensively. His website lists close to fifty venues, starting in 2004. His work has been featured in the magazines *Black and White* and *Photo Art International* (France), and can be found in numerous corporate and private collections.

Since 1998, Igor has lived in the in the quiet suburban town of Lawrenceville in central New Jersey with his wife Olga, who supports and shares his passion for photography.

CPSIA information can be obtained
at www.ICGtesting.com
Printed in the USA
FFOW03n1014060814
6711FF